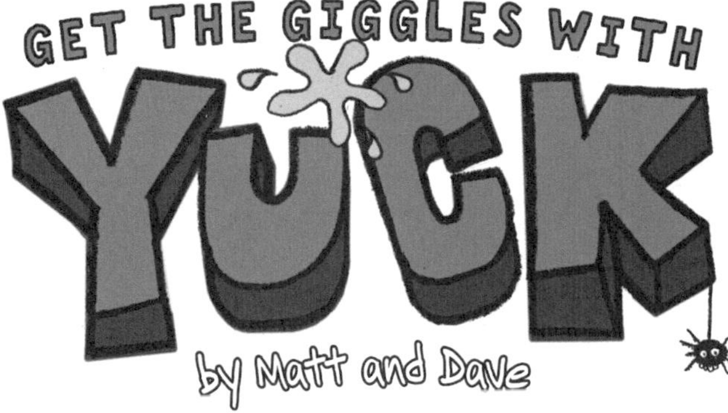

Yuck's Smelly Socks

Illustrated by Nigel Baines

Chapters Page

1
A Cheesy Choice

Yuck opened his sock drawer. It was full of socks: long socks, short socks, school socks and sports socks, but **ALL** of them were **CLEAN**.

Yuck sniffed. They smelled daisy-fresh from Mum's **SUPERSUDS** washing powder. Clean socks are no fun at all, Yuck thought.

From under his bed, Yuck pulled out a pair of old, smelly socks: the last smelly pair he had left. He pressed them to his nose. "Mmmmm … dirty, crusty, cheesy socks! That's better!"

Yuck put them on.

Just then, Mum poked her nose round the door. "Yuck, have you got clean socks on today?"

"Yes, Mum," Yuck replied.

"Good, I don't want you wearing smelly socks any more. It's revolting."

"I know, Mum," Yuck said, quickly slipping his shoes on.

He ran downstairs to the front door, where his sister Polly Princess was waiting for him.

"Hurry up, Yuck," Polly said.

Yuck and Polly left together for school. Polly coughed as she walked.

"**PHWOAR**, Yuck!" she said. "Your socks stink!"

Yuck decided that when he was **EMPEROR OF EVERYTHING**, all his socks would be smelly.

He would be the King of Foot Cheese and Toe Jam, and everyone would come from miles around to smell his stinky feet. It would be the **LAW**!

At school, Yuck sat at the back of the class with his shoes off and his feet on the desk.

The smell of foot cheese drifted across the room. Everyone looked round, their noses twitching.

"**PHWOOAARR**, Yuck!" they yelled. "Your socks stink of **CHEESE!**"

Yuck's teacher pinched her nose. "You're not to wear smelly socks in my class!" she said.

PHWoOOAAARRRR!
COUGH SPLUTTER

That evening, Polly told on Yuck. "Mum, Yuck's been wearing smelly socks today," she said.

"Is that true, Yuck?" Mum asked.

"Of course not," Yuck replied. Quickly, he raced upstairs, took his socks off and hid them under his bed.

Mum poked her head round his door. She eyed Yuck's bare feet suspiciously. "If I find out that you've got smelly socks in here, they're going straight in the wash."

Yuck couldn't bear the thought of Mum washing his smelly socks. He needed a plan ...

What if I make them **SUPER** smelly? he thought. What if I make my socks **SO** smelly that not even Mum's **SUPERSUDS** washing powder can get them clean?

First, he would need some stinky ingredients.

Yuck waited until the coast was clear, then he crept outside to the rubbish bin. He found a mouldy ham sandwich and half a banana.

Then, from the fridge, he fetched a block of cheese and a hard-boiled egg. He raced back to his room and picked up a baseball bat.

BANG! BANG! SPLAT!

Yuck bashed the ingredients into a mush, then scooped it into his socks.

He pulled the socks on and wiggled his toes. Mmmm, lovely and mushy, he thought. Now to let it all stew.

That night, Yuck slept with his socks on, and they grew more and more smelly. He dreamed he was in a cheese factory where blocks of cheese were passing by on a conveyor belt.

He was Chief Cheesy Hole Maker, poking holes in the cheese with his toes.

2
A Whacky Whiff

The next day at school, Yuck's socks smelled so bad that he was made to stand outside the classroom!

At lunchtime, from the school canteen, he fetched two fish fingers, a handful of cabbage and a bowl of baked beans. He mashed them into his socks, and all day long they squelched as he walked.

At home that evening, Yuck took a cheese sandwich to his room. He peeled it open and wiped the buttered bread over his feet. He broke the cheese into lumps and wedged them between his toes.

Then Yuck lay in bed with his socks on, letting it all stew ...

That night, Yuck dreamed he went to cheese school. The whole school was made of cheese. The doors were made of cheese, the desks were made of cheese and even the teachers were made of cheese!

3
Pizza Pong

The following morning, on the way to school, Yuck passed two dogs that were sniffing one another's bottoms. They sniffed his socks, then barked and ran away.

Awesome! Yuck thought. My socks now smell worse than a dog's bottom!

When Yuck arrived at school, he saw a sign on the classroom door saying: NO SMELLY SOCKS. So he sneaked to the school pond and filled his socks with slime and frogspawn. A frog hopped out from one of them. "Ribbit!" it said.

Yuck wiggled his toes and the frog licked them, covering them in slippery slobber.

That evening, Yuck sneaked a slice of pizza and some cheesy chips from the kitchen, and raced to his room.

He pushed the pizza into his socks, getting the gooey topping deep under his toenails. Then he sprinkled the cheesy chips in, too.

He heard Polly bang on his door.

"What's that awful smell, Yuck?" she asked.

"Nothing," Yuck replied.

"But I can smell something through the keyhole."

Yuck giggled. "It must be your breath." He hopped into bed to let his socks stew.

That night, Yuck dreamed he was paddling in the sea. He dipped his feet in the water, and all the fish jumped out, shouting, "PHWOARR! CHEESY!"

4
Supersud Surprise

When Yuck woke up, he lifted his blanket and a cheesy cloud erupted from underneath.

Fantastic! he thought. His socks were now the stinkiest, honkiest, **SMELLIEST** socks **EVER!**

His socks smelled so bad that, at school, they wafted cheesy smells along the corridor. Children were coughing and spluttering, running for cover.

A cheesy cloud began to fill the school. The principal came to see what all the fuss was.

"Yuck! Are those your socks that smell?" he asked. But as the principal spoke, the cheesy gas wafted into his mouth.

"**UUURRGH!**" he cried. "Evacuate the building!"

Everyone ran to the playground and Yuck heard the sound of sirens. He saw flashing lights as fire engines, ambulances and police cars arrived to deal with the emergency.

That evening, Mum got quite a surprise when she opened the front door ...

and saw Yuck with a fire-fighter holding Yuck's smelly socks in a plastic bag.

"I think these need washing, Madam," he said.

Yuck stepped inside and Mum closed the door. "You naughty boy, Yuck! I told you not to wear smelly socks any more. These are going in the washing machine **NOW!**"

Yuck followed Mum to the kitchen. She opened the washing machine and threw his smelly socks inside.

"My SUPERSUDS washing powder will soon get them daisy-fresh," she said.

We'll see about that, Yuck thought. He had an idea. "Mum, wait a minute. I've got some more."

Yuck ran upstairs and took all the clean socks from his drawer. He carried them down and popped them in the washing machine with his smelly socks.

"You can turn it on now, Mum," said Yuck.

Mum poured in the **SUPERSUDS** washing powder and turned the washing machine to **FULL POWER**.

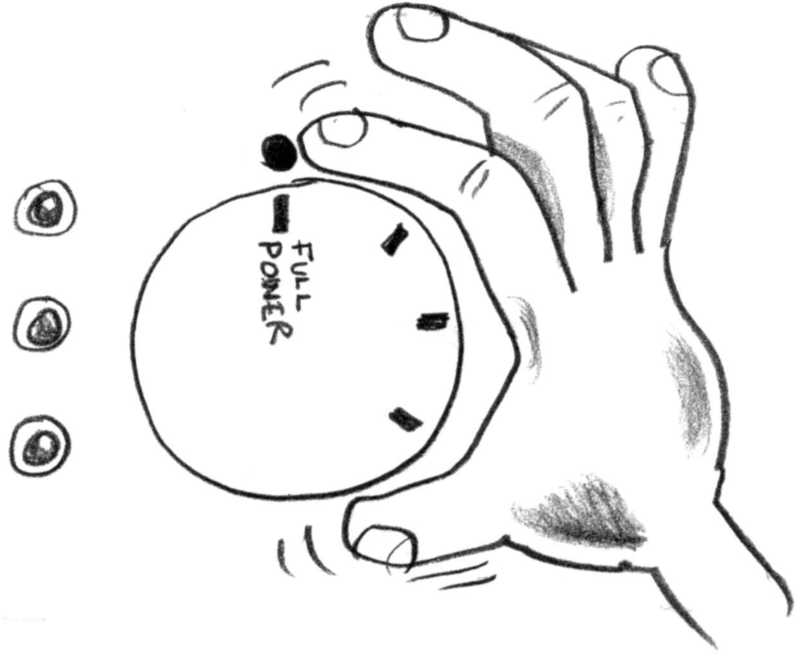

Yuck watched as the washing machine started to whirl. The **SUPERSUDS** foamed and the washing machine made noises, growling and groaning.

Yuck's socks spun faster and faster.

The **SUPERSUDS** and his smelly socks were locked in battle.

Yuck could see cheese, frogspawn, pizza and chips spinning round and round.

The washing machine gurgled loudly and the **SUPERSUDS** frothed.

Polly ran into the kitchen. "What's that noise?" she asked.

"I'm washing Yuck's socks," Mum told her.

At that moment there was a huge **RUMBLE**, then a loud **BLURGH**!

The washing machine burst open, belching cheesy gas.

"**UUURRRGGGHHH!**" Mum and Polly cried.

Yuck smiled. His smelly socks had beaten the washing powder!

Yuck reached in and pulled out all his socks: long socks, short socks, school socks and sports socks, and now **ALL** of them were smelly!

"Mmmm, that's more like it," Yuck said. "Smelly socks are the best!"